I0796095

Dear Birch,

Dear Birch,

Margaret Christakos

Palimpsest Press
1171 Eastlawn Ave.
Windsor, Ontario. N8S 3J1
www.palimpsestpress.ca

Printed and bound in Canada
Cover design and book typography by Ellie Hastings
Edited by Jim Johnstone

Palimpsest Press would like to thank the Canada Council for the Arts and the Ontario Arts Council for their support of our publishing program. We also acknowledge the assistance of the Government of Ontario through the Ontario Book Publishing Tax Credit.

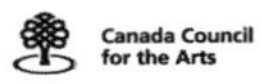

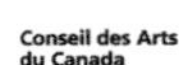

LIBRARY AND ARCHIVES CANADA CATALOGUING IN PUBLICATION

Title: Dear birch / Margaret Christakos.
Names: Christakos, Margaret, author.
Description: Poems.
Identifiers: Canadiana (print) 20210101016
Canadiana (ebook) 20210101024

ISBN 9781989287682 (softcover) | ISBN 9781989287699 (EPUB)
ISBN 9781989287705 (kindle) | ISBN 9781989287712 (PDF)

classification: LCC PS8555.H675 D43 2021 | DDC C811/.54—dc23 *T*

Table of Contents

O, the colour all around was joystruck or caused her/him
to become so

from "Retreat Diary," 2003

Time tall in you like every erectile birch still untickled

but all green leaves flutter quill quaver & make a
semaphore of a thousand short right stories

from "Waiting," 2005

Enough I have had
Of my paper-skinned nature.

from "Birch," 2009

Aug 24

She is a diarist, & as such wants
to remember thoughts & events she has lived,

especially the delicate events & contradictory thoughts she
perceives herself to be hearing & watching. She

is reporting on her own attentions, while feeling
the sensations spring from her entire body. She

senses you shiver there, twelve feet ahead, beyond
the iron tabletop. She tries to define why

she comes here, sitting & growling, when it
is not exactly pleasant. It aches in ways

that still need naming. The ache reaches, high
into your branches, brightening at the grey-white tissue

you like to wave around. The day ends,
night occurs, & she returns, with her coffee,

her notebook. She greets you without sound &,
in turn, you are perennially vibrating, like a

white mammal with a matte soft coat, or
the memory of shark, airborne.

    She keeps trying. What is it she would
say about her practice, if a thin margin

invites the right hand to scrawl a note
or two? She pileates the bark of her

fatigue today. Go ahead, she waves.

All right. She *does* make poems, & tries
to build stories or narratives that bounce into

the established limit-categories of these genres, but primarily,
if she has to name it — & she

does want to name it — most of her
writing, when she really feels herself to be

writing's sucked straight from the inner chamber of
her thinking about what she sees, hears, detects,

gathers & brings into relationship. It is a
mode of noticing that she is alive at

this particular time & place, on a specific
day, with a recordable weather (nature's), dreams (the

previous night's) & moods (her own, once awake),
using her senses to probe & name states

of being going on around her, the setting,
sound, feel, place & space she finds herself

within, & of sporting these recognitions into units
of composition that often challenge capacities of poetic

line & prose narrative sentence. Her diaristic prose
handles grammar as if it is a set

of nets allowing the ping-pong sponginess of many
small balls to ricochet within its open fretwork

of containment — at any moment one of the
balls might erupt out of bounds & break

the arc of all of them. Her sentence
is kinesis, a yard, a patio, train track,

a kitchen. She thinks herself a juggler — an
improviser. Writing is improvisation.

So she could reframe her initial declaration about
keeping a diary; now she wants to say

she makes notes on what is noticed &,
also, unnoticed. She puts herself to task at

trying to notice inner & outer events simultaneously.

For the ten minutes you had seemed invisible
you caught up on some sleep; now she

is watching you again & listening. The cicada
buzzing this morning is ostentatious, & so is

the vibrational numbness in her hand as she
tries to keep this pen moving.

She *is* writing with a pen — this one,
bright orange with a white flare-shaped flourish &,

in modernist black type, hotelalma.ca emblazoned on its
belly (probably where she roosted for the weekend,

Athens, 2012, before the Classical Tour to Delphi,
Epidaurus, Olympia…) — in a plain blue-lined Hilroy notebook.

She writes densely on every line when she's
in a terse mood tethering herself to detail

& urgent desire; on every second line when
she senses a certain lyrical liftoff is occurring

akin to flying a kite & running alone
on the beach below it unwrapping extra lengths

of distance so the kite can soar where
it wishes. (Like a cyclops, you point out

that this text so far's on every line.)

These are two of the paces & textures
of composition she can name — but there are

others. There's the situation where she feels dumb,
without words, all latticed in shades of flickering

hopelessness — here, even though she is nowhere near
a lake, sometimes a phrase washes upon shore

from under the dank dock: She doesn't want
to get too close to the fragment, respecting

it's already a wet broken thing lucky to
have survived at all. She tries to find

it a warm burrow on this page, with
plenty of plain solace around it. There's the

trick-juggle of turning four balls into sixteen &
making them criss-cross & rotate sideways & giving

each the slight weight of a single alphabetic
letter. Letters spring, like sprigs of ivy, or

like your bouncing leaf bunches. & There is
pure moaning & drivel, which she usually erases

or scribbles over; no one needs spend their
fragrant lunch hour editing it for free.

There are many acoustic spaces to write within,
the mall, basement, elevator, streetcar, coffee shop, urban

river bank after her long bike ride when
the body is completely drunk on wind, public

libraries where everyone is equally drunk on social
silence. There is the onset & sudden ending

of various sounds — a shimmer of having heard
something finish, which to her always feels akin

to having outlived catastrophe & being one of
the imperilled left to continue. New sounds begin —

they always do. She senses you agree, with
breeze a pink whistle at your neckline.

Other people & creatures are always present, often
just as sounds of their moving or mode

of being. Waiting is a state of noticing
that being alone is an incomplete observation of

the actual world. The longer she listens, the
more accompanied, & even crowded, she feels: She

never entirely likes the residual bubbles of presence
& infinite expansion on a scale of sentience —

bristling ant, brown flock cawing in a grey
cloud, constructing crews on hot roofs three doors

away, a yellow sock seeping air into a
garden's curb, the mangy mute cat paw poking

under her fence. She has to leave writing,
sometimes, to resume the relief of solitude. Then

sitting beneath your arms works like a charm.

To make a diary entry is to forestall
calling it anything else. It's not a nine-month

project that deserves twelve thousand dollars; it's not
an idea for marketable fiction. Not fame in

its dressing gown. It's a specific, internal, interval
during which she is alive & still keeps

access to the mechanics of drawing down, or
up, or in, language, & can make something

from it, within it, & for it, too.
She can convene language to meet other language

it has not yet met — maybe — & other
times she just doesn't want the pressure of

being in that room, with those awkward bodies
who can't think of a word to say

to any other body.

When she writes in her diary her whole
body is making an effort to recognize being

connected to the act of thinking, or, her
whole body is thinking about events happening at

the same moment within & without what she
thinks of as herself. This last sentence admittedly

a disappointment. Dry, brittle, lanky, wrought. She can
get rid of or keep listening to it;

writing is editing, selecting, commissioning a tone, fussing
that she's about to lose the kite in

a heavier-than-expected yank of wind. Or, the wind
drops, & the kite thuds to the beach,

like a squirrel, knocked out.

She has just left this text, to move
a load of towels from washer to dryer,

to check if the washer has flooded, as
it did last week, if the kids are

up, to get more coffee despite her doctor's
suggestion she stick to one cup a day,

for now, to see. Her legs & guts
are settling back into this iron patio chair,

there are low voices in the back lane
at the entrance to the cool craft brewery

as they sweep before opening (people can, from
11 on, judge a $12 "flight" of four

unique homemade ales — curators, then, not mere early
morning drinkers). On the back gate, sunlight is

skittishly permuting the shapes of your leaves to
tender spasms of shadow. It looks as though

there must be a soundscape to transcribe, but
all the bird chirps & churning accelerating car

engines are separate events. The gate's shadow-play is
its own soundless incident that she must use

her gaze to experience & she knows you
are listening.

When she reads over this diary entry she
fills it with her own voice, auralizing how

her speech sounds in her head & also
then reading the sentences out loud, hearing her

voice in & among the cicada buzz, the
brewery's air conditioner, a set of tools being

tapped & jostled, the GO train approaching from
the west, a repaired streetcar wailing back onto

the Gerrard track. Partial memories of the dream
she had flicker — she was climbing a sizeable

mountainside, as if underground, in a tunnelled chute
with a weak headlamp soaking the space directly

above her, where various thickly leaved bushes pressed
onto her bare arms, & she could sense

her boots slipping against gravelly soil. From the
thicket of darkness above her left brow leans

a large dark-grey mountain cat, first its imperious
snout, its steel-black eyes & flitting ears, hump

of its pure-muscle foreleg stepping directly, now, toward
her gaze, & she suffocates a scream &

freezes the panic of her instinct icily observing
it, or her; how it seems specifically now

a she-panther, tersing her indigo shoulder to pass
fully around her, skin grazed by fur as

she struggles against dissembling. She feels decreasing suction
as the cat goes behind her, on her

path, & instead resumes the job of being
more afraid of the black mouth of the

tunnel up the mountainside ahead of her than
she is of the wild carnivore sheltered now

beneath her & her desire. Like the soundless
shadows, images from dreams hover as miraculous material.

She is likely never to forget the apparition
of that particular big feline, & how intimate

an idea they were for that brief dramatic
spectacle. It was a virtual encounter as real

to her as the red-backed spider she just
brushed in a tiny panic off her calf.

Both are precisely present on this patio, at
this moment, with your limbs & the cicadas

& machines & rustling wind & all other
simultaneous bodies at all scales of sentience.

        There is always so much going on that
a diary entry yearns to ignore at least

half, because chiefly, she needs to hear herself
think, to bring her own being into language.

Otherwise both the being & the language seem
tenuous & escapable. Why does she exist? What

language trick makes these transmissions even possible? How
can anyone, with their own quixotic being, run

into her voice in a dark tunnel &,
with their own voice, connect brutally for a

second & then slide past, both released with
only an imprint of happenstance & a shred

of story to record in the ping-pong grammar
of narrative? You may agree, dear birch, or

not; she hopes you will escort the morning
of effort, the noon of flagging off near

to a nap, the afternoon glass of coffee
& ice.

She doesn't know why she guesses that a
diary entry is a worthy act — in 2018 —

in an era of digital encryption that replaces
speech utterly — but she does. It's the panther

that stops her pulse, & the pantomime of
mood that interests her intellect. There it is.

It's a form of cinema she steps into,
as an improviser of memory, of thoughts &

events, & of noticing.

Aug 19

Then, as a long & slow second thought,
she properly takes you in. Your zinging cicada

trill. Your outfurled flags of foliage. The neighbour
babies's large grunts, like garden toads, palpable through

their shared fence. In the kitchen behind her,
her own twins are in their home shorts,

swilling warm salt water across the healing sockets
where their wisdom teeth were tugged out three

days ago. Houseflies & moths flit in her
periphery. Your special vitamin is a quiet patience

for reading. You line yourself up to enter
her, radiant syrup, supplemental toxin. She is becoming

intoxicated.

Aug 20

When writing returns to her solitary mind without
precipitative audience through social media, she feels... *little*.

She feels confused. Imagines forward to a reader
if & when these phrases are lifted into

a public space. She is unmoored. She's on
hold — missing all the pleasures of feeling instantaneously

read, that are intense & addicting. The congratulatory
recognition of all the flickerish signs of being

influential: the hearts, the checkmarks, licorice comments, the
thumbs-ups, giving a chill sense of being seen

at work by colleagues — a forum so completely
missing in the longer time scale of writing

labour. But maybe there's a whole battery of
questions she's not asking of herself. A way

of thinking about the texts she is making...
&, then, *aha*, she falls away to mindlessly

checking Facebook and Twitter.

Refocusing. Gathering into her senses.

Naming & transcribing the sounds she hears — the
social processes in play. The neighbour's tenant laughing

& cooing on her cellphone on the fence's
other side to the right, the woman named

L adjusting & hoisting the babies's double carriage
to the left, heard across the fence. Social

witness & congress of a different kind. Her
awareness & mapping of the weather, the movement

of leaves on your slightly swaying branches. Flickering
of shadow & sunlight, chute exhaust of the

coffee roastery's air conditioner. Her hair unfurling from
a self-coiled bun sliding like a squirrel tail

onto the back of her neck. Voices from
the brewery employees across the lane, & eastward,

a more distant scrape of shovel & women's
laughter. A rising jangle of cicada song, or

physical friction, however they make this strange electric
buzz as a colony all at once. Nearby

smooth suction of a door into its frame,
the metal stopper engaging. Quiet, dormant, eternal, black

cellphone gleaming on the patio table in front,
a book she's awaiting to return to, secondary

pencil & calendar, her coffee cup, her numb
buzzing fingers gripping the pen she holds — so

like the cicada sound, sensation nervous in her,
jostling accoutrement. Her neighbour now sitting almost silent

except for fork tines or scoop of spoon
tapping a ceramic bowl or plate, indicating she

is quietly eating, maybe reading as well, perhaps
noticing *her* figure as a collage of visual

shapes, through her peripheral view of the "neighbour's
yard" — this patio & you, dear birch. Inside

the house are two of her adult children,
one in the basement adjusting sound levels, making

music out of beats, beats out of music,
& one upstairs working, typing, planning, cataloguing her

extraordinary photographs, moving in her many directions, at
once.

Inevitably, now, she gets agitated — checks online again.
Instead of this writing, she begins to crave

reading, considers books she has been reading, Camilla
Gibb's *This is Happy*, Roxane Gay's *Hunger*, Maria

Mutch's *Know the Night*, her friend's manuscript mourning
her sister with Down Syndrome, Vaclev Havel's essays,

all first-person narratives except for Solnit's brilliant bio
of Muybridge, but even that, strongly driven by

the writer's interest in making sense of Muybridge's
life, inner & outer, in tandem.

Why, now, why does the memoir genre grab
her? She makes a list: For personality — movement

of specific mind in specific circumstances; For voice —
an experience of hearing the elongated speech act,

almost as reactive to the sound bite as
Netflix dramatic series now are to the fragment

on YouTube & social media; Continuity; A movement
of consciousness & a sense of the body

being physically located in real & persuasive spaces;
A representation of how life is an amalgamation

of the self experiencing new encounters & therefore
inventing new narrative testimonial about experience; Unique
story;

A mirror for the reader's own self-narrative of
memory, where she was when the memoirist was

at or in her own life; The sense
of being in time, being in the past

which can be described narratively & being in
the present which can be characterized in relation

to the past & potential future; For language,
writing & interpretation.

Just staying with the writing process is hard.
Years ago she would have written ten or

twelve pages all about her feelings. Now she
can only write when her feelings are dispensed

with. She just walks or sits with her
feelings — she rides a bike with her feelings.

She knows they are tempestuous & vacillating — this
leads her to search the word "changeable" &

consider vocabulary for this idea of how her
feelings shift & transform into others; How she

becomes so associated with one, or two weirdly
sutured, & has to wait for the system

to permute to another, especially feelings of pain,
loss, desire, wishfulness, refusal, yearning, overattachment.
She has

to wait to let it shift to a
more flexible, less attached investment especially in the

love object. So much lifework in this gradual
unhinging.

Aug 21

A steady, determined rain that began earlier while
she was sleeping. Now gathering intensity drumming down

on the grass & roads, gardens & rooftops.
Will it leak into the basement, again, be

wicked up & sponged in by the carpet?

G here last night for dinner which they
had on the patio, a perfect calm cool

evening & their conversation was continuous. At some
points they spoke over each other, on her

part, trying to insert her own perspective or
stories occasionally overshadowed by G's narrative. She was

aware of the weakness in her own voice,
a dullness, slow to wit, stumbling at points

on her word choice, a sense she was
too emotional & exposed, not good enough at

decorating her disclosures with style & irony.

Broke off to read R's message again responding
to hers — she's proposing getting together tonight. Her

gut is saying... two contradictory things — one: *Yes*;
two: *No*. She's so not a ruminator, so

not a dedicated replay artist. She lives by
a momentum to move on, even if the

moving on involves bending the truth or covering
her ass. She so wants to test out

her own capacity to stand up for herself
against R, to not be erasive & compliant —

but all this moral language also shuts her
up in her own process. She doesn't believe

anymore in "winning the argument" as a way
to be in relationship, but it's left her

strategy-poor in sticking with what she wants &
how she agrees to be treated. If she's

going to stop seeing R there's no need
to be nasty, fire-tongued. Best to just say

with affection, *Thanks for the memories*. At many
depths that's where she's at.

But by other scores — maybe a poor apology
is the only apology R does. Maybe she

has to read under its thin bravado to
find the message she's also sending, one that

says she hopes to see her. But why?
When she is so preoccupied with seeking others,

& finding them, for fleeting, unattached sex. The
point is that, when they grow conflicted in

any way, she maintains a transactional ambivalence with
her, no matter how long they continue to

see each other & how much history they've
shared.

These incriminations by X toward her really did
their work — she bears a strong shame at

being a bitch, being erratic, mean, vindictive, unbending,
violent even, being called *crazy*. This dismissal of

her deeper emotional bond with him was meant
to free her for her new attachment, so

she could go forward into a clean, new,
untarnished partnership & be done with all the

stained memories of their union. But X did
really love her, over many years, & she

also entered into a loyal committed bond with
him. This is not the direction things are

taking with R — it's not a slow, somewhat
painful motion toward attachment. Or if it is,

her barriers are much more acute. It might
be R isn't capable of showing or feeling

more than she feels now for her. She
may be too damaged, too self-preserving (or uniformly

lust-driven).

One thing's for sure — she's not sitting with
a notebook writing through her thoughts on this

or any other emotional identity issue. G may
well be, at least in their workday-sideline thinking

about, possibly replaying, how their date was totally
platonic — disappointing & flattening for them both. They

had talked so much about their families &
siblings, & she talked about X, & G

talked about two of their major past partners,
how both those breakups involved them feeling unseen,

unmet & helplessly resolved to pursue a necessary
change for their own good. She admired G's

clarity & this insistence on the future as
better adventure. Still — she thinks there's something deeper

she's not working through yet with her relationship
to R. It is her own tactic of

having kept a safety loop of non-monogamy during
her partnership with X. She is sleeping with

someone who needs & wants to have unfettered
access to sexual experience with anyone she wants,

in encounters that are anonymous & singular. Somehow,
she explains, they are not intimate, whereas their

connection is intimate, or was intimate. & The
hierarchy has appealed to her & made sense,

since she doesn't want a more defined bond.
But she does feel threatened & debased by

all of her sexual seeking. Partly it makes
her distrust her, not know how to call

her on being less than honest or on
sidling over disclosures unless she asks for information

directly about what she's doing. That's a major
tactic for her — don't ask, don't tell.

The main thing for her to remember, though,
is that the third anniversary today of her

mother's death may be an important signal to
her, that letting go & saying goodbye is

pith of life & part of facing change.
She has found a need in herself for

the poetic or ceremonial, an extra-resonant "logic" guiding
her emotional choices. Today is probably a good

day to decide to stand by her own
dignity & let R know she's grateful for

what they've shared & also realistic about the
limits that seem to be hampering their connection

from getting deeper. But even in writing this
she feels squeamish & sad — she doesn't want

to lose her. She does feel there's potential,
or she thinks she does, or she wishes

there will be. It's so hard to stay
honest when it seems like a choice to

say farewell, instead of when leavetaking is happening
without her consent, as in losing her mother,

& her father, & X.

In the evening, after a late August rainstorm
blew through the dinner hour, R first texts

to say she can come earlier, & can
be aware of her mother's death-iversary; & Then,

once she's confirmed, triggering the sequence of events
involved in preparing, perhaps, or, likely, to receive

an estranged lover, to argue & then to
reconcile, R texts she's had a professional crisis

to solve, that, first, will put her in
a scurrilous mood &, second, will stop her

from coming altogether, & third, that besides, now
she's fallen ill, with a very sore stomach

& "feels ungainly." R's masterfully offloaded any &
all responsibility to make up. She sends R

the least quarrelsome reply possible, brief, neutral, helping
her to brush them both away.

So then begins her reaction, the action she
takes in order not to feel utterly erased.

She settles into recreating a new Match profile,
the site she originally met R through, then

left over a year ago sensing there was
no desire in her to find alternative hook

ups; despite R's activity, she was feeling gratified
& excited with her. After refurbishing her online

ad, she starts browsing, & finds so many
of the same prospects who were there a

year ago, in particular another lover she'd enjoyed
for five or six dates until it was

clear she was a raging sex addict — &
(surprise, surprise) R herself, saying she's 55 looking

for those 34 to 49 (she's 51). Most
of her other details are as they were

a year and a half ago. Her chest
closes up. She looks at a few more

profiles, then dumps & deletes the whole thing.
Who needs the clutter of restless cruising?

But somehow the whole experience looses her from
caring so much or feeling as badly as

she had been feeling. She thinks about being
in charge of her own next steps. If

she enables R to persist with the distance
she's allowing between them, not even calling, using

only curt texts to claim participation in this
slow, quiet fight — if she doesn't take on

the role of verbal facilitator — she will get
what R's proposing: *Let's get this over with.*

Aug 22

Awaking into the resolve of a new day,
one with a smoke-coloured moist sky & breeze

rushing through your canopy creating a pleasurable field
of sonic caresses both calming & inciting; it

drenches her inner hearing & makes her brain
tissue bloom, her lungs reach up through her

esophagus (do lungs & esophagus connect? She's not
even sure) & feel stroked expansively. There's a

scent to this wind as well, laced throughout
your green flutter & a stirring exertion of

the body as a vital wave. Also, chimes
are set off by the breeze, toggling a

singable pitch in little magical bell-phrases. It's beautiful
out here today. & There, the yanked squeal

of subway cars in the yard beyond train
tracks, the incoming GO train arriving & passing

in sudden shudders across a brown squirrel's fence-post
vista so she stops in her muscular alarm

& freezes, *WTF* etched on her immobilized brow.
There are the impetuous car horns burping up

from Gerrard & a neighbour's electronic phone alarm
calling for a body to touch the device

& press it to her ear & begin
listening & talking. She can't tell you how

her heart would seize if someone came in
the night & decapitated you, dear birch, &

your reign over the patio, if someone should
enter to burglar your branches or, worst, slice

your trunk & grind the spine of it —
she would vomit. She would rage. What a

tree provisions her cannot be conducted by air
alone, cannot be restaged by a greenhouse sapling

slipped into the massive root cavity that would
be left torn open if you, dear birch,

were routed. She prays there's no morning where
she wakes to such a scene.

She wonders this because, yesterday, another Manitoba
maple
was "removed" from the lane, east of here,

a huge arching mother moose of a structure,
gracefully reaching out over the drive, shuddering along

her whole height & width as the gorgeous
wind passed through her, & she was chopped

into logs, dispatched by truck away from the
neighbourhood & this morning there is a gaping

aeration in the canopy — a blank full of
silent air — a patch of sky unmottled &

ungirded by stems & leaves & limbs, a
general further lightness in the sky here from

her vantage. But the tree's void is a
gesticulation of space that has capacity to erase

& make invisible the reality that existed hours
earlier & which now she must decide to

remember or let slide into the continuity of
the present.

It seems she needs to have a book
called *Wind*, the wind (with a short i),

which is a winding (with a long i)
of the senses into reception. She can't live

without wind. Or, a headstone, *M, who needed*
the wind to survive. O wind! Dear wind.

Feeling winded — such a strange use of the
word wind to confer that state of being

short of breath, instead of bathed in it.

Winded, which sounds like "wind dead" & "win
did", a previous state of having won, of

being victorious, or declaration or refutation of the
fact of having won — *I did so win!*

I did! Also, *it was the wind did*
it, it's the wind! The beguiling gusts of

"wand wend wind wond wund wynd" & "wind
dinw dniw" all askew, as a poet wrote

online one day. The wind that makes movement
possible, say, for the Greeks in their boats,

how Artemis returns wind to let Agamemnon sail
to war, after he has paid with his

daughter's sacrifice, who turns (probably) into a young
deer & wisps away into forest, who rotates

into a blur of disappearing most exemplified by
how the wind moves.

There is also how varied wind is, in
all seasons, how trees wear the wind &

are dressed & undressed by the wind.

There is the terrible slipperiness of wind. There
is the challenge of photographing the wind in

action, as it is spirit, invisible, can only
be seen by what it does to objects

& matter. There is the history of harnessing
wind to use as an energy source for

machine-driven production.

There's diagonally descending tornadoes, downbursts &
side-slanting windstorms.
There's the subtle dance of utensils moving in

shadow as wind produces a visual cinema of
motion.

There's the wind's refusal of stillness, time never
stopping, of tools and weathered gear astir toward

utility.

Wind is breath, is life. Wind is the
starter as it's suckled into infant lungs — suction

that starts a life.

Wind is outside an architectural structure. It can
be synthesized by fans & machines as "moving

air", but real wind is a natural force
that belongs to & constitutes being in the

outside. Wind is invisible unless it is loaded
with matter it carries, when it can become

smoke, or stain, or broth, waves of awe.

Wind moves satin like thinking. Wind can seem
to be absent but it returns just as

thoughts are inspired as the motion of moving
from stillness to new concept.

Wind is an equalizer, able to salve &
wreck rich & poor with equal neutrality.

Wind sweeps you somewhere else. You pray for
wind to move you when you are paralyzed

by inaction. You beg for wind to stay
present enough to infuse the body & mind

with muscle & urge but not so strong
that it blows you away.

Now she sees so clearly, so predictably, that
her love of you, dear birch, is also

a love of wind, love of interrelation of
wind in trees, trees in wind.

Little winds & large winds. Breezes & storms.
Life, death.

Whitman's observation of a leaf of grass; How
does he portray it as in motion? How

soon does this happen in the observation? Breath
of life, of course.

The end of wind. Wind's end. Wind winding
down.

Windows, which keep out wind or calibrate how
much wind gets in.

Wind machines, wind tunnels, wind damage, wind force.

Wind in winter.

Remembering wind. Making wind visible. Her body bathing
in wind.

Aug 23

Soft light, lemon, with a leading edge of
the cold burst of a fridge releasing its

air into a room. She sneezes & resneezes
at pollen seeping. Contemplates the rejections she's received

almost weekly, from Canadian poetry journals she used
to be welcomed by, to be given kind

of a salute in correspondence, openly flattered. Now
there's nothing personalized about it — a Submittable form

letter from an editorial board reminding everyone how
overworked & taxed it is, how not to

become glum at the rebuff. One, two, three.
This morning makes four.

          & She is catching scenes from the seemingly
lengthy dreaming she did last night in between

spurts of wakefulness, during which she tossed her
history with R into a multiple-choice quiz box

of what ifs & whatevers. Her skin still
agitated, itchy. In the dream portion she'd developed

a festering patch of flesh below her right
knee, on the pliable pouch of skin about

three inches farther down, visibly hosting some variant
of bright infection — so yes, an exaggeration of

distracting sensation, but also allegory of the small
(or massive) cold sore she'd had healing on

her lower nostril when they last saw each
other & R said she'd changed her mind,

just then, didn't care to sleep with her,
worried she was technically contagious, that she was

(presumably) compromising her chances for dating others, in
some way.

That around-midnight conflict set off waves of
woundedness
in her, tide of seduction undoing itself &

here it is weeks & they've only managed
a broken telegraphy of malign text messages. It

could be 1872 with a postman & horse,
before it was possible to see the individual

frame of all four hooves in the air,
suspended.

In the dreaming & the wakefulness she was
running over the long list of encounters they'd

shared & assessing each for its pattern of
callous, rough-about-the-edges nonchalance, or even moreso,
R's *non-chaleur*.

By four a.m. she had amassed enough dark
purple file folders of evidence for the prosecution

that she was given leave to drop into
the full REM-driven dream of the skin-wound &,

now, that's much of what she's ghosted by
here on the patio with its lemon soft-noonlight

& released-seal wafts of cool air, its lime-sour
hints of pollen, & her sneezing, brief but

violent, where it feels as though this moment
she is wracked in hysterical possession by a

wild being. There: If she's going to go
Victorian, why not deep-dive? Why not be predated

& possessed?

She almost wants to be knocked out of
a nest, or shunted off a high branch,

like that drunk woman off a cruise ship,
or the auburn squirrel in Monarch Park yesterday,

that dropped at the speed of a small
body pushed off a bank tower & cold-stopped

flat & prostrate on the hard ground about
five metres from where she was seated taking

a selfie amid reams of photographs of the
shadow-dappled huge oaks at noonday. The squirrel literally

made a THUD as its whole figure, with
tail extended straight out behind, hit the soil.

It had plunged at least thirty feet. For
a moment, then about three minutes more, it

did not move & she thought she'd witnessed
a brutal incontroversion of natural order — a BLAM

or KAZAM finale for this inconsequential rodent's lifespan.
It lay sprawled in a flattened stasis. It

was dead. Had to be.

        Then it twitched & heaved itself back to
the base of the tree it fell from,

a distance less than two metres, & stopped
again, dead still, then writhed slightly & moved

its four small clawed feet onto the root's
hump & yanked itself vertical onto the dark-brown

bark runnels of the trunk &, again, froze,
inverted straight up, seemingly dying or dead. It

felt to her she watched a creature hemorrhage
internally, its unburst fur contour a russet disguise

& a ruse, just a brief interval before
the whole life of the animal would spill-out

as a hot red microburst. But it didn't.
It survived, grimping upward in short climbs then

recuperative rests, to get back to the branch
it had originally fallen from. She watched it

ascend, nose-first, tail flagging, all the way up.

        Later, after she picked up her refurbished bike
from the store called CyclePath (aha-ha), she rode

west across Danforth to find some lunch — spinach
pie or souvlaki, she hadn't decided — & steered

directly by a large raccoon body violently left
on the paved road, its plentiful guts dumped

to view, with swirling knots of intestines, punched
snout glued askew to the tar. It was

a macabre flash in her vision; She pedalled
past & felt sick, felt her lungs wheeze,

cheeks gape. Kept riding until a pizza shop
came into view & she thought, *Fuck it,*

I"ll just have a slice here, a block
from Jones & Danforth, & parked the as-if-new

beautifully working bike, & clattered into the small
parlour. On the oversized monitor above the group

of tables the previous night's news was backfilling,
& she read how ten hours earlier at

approximately this same intersection a man had been
shot in the head & left for dead

on the sidewalk, outside a sports bar, that
the suspect had mercifully been arrested but that

an accomplice might still be lurking, that was
all the information police would release. No word

if the assassination was gang-related, or involved drugs
or some deep-churning private vendetta, or a misspoken

dare, or churlish slur.

Sometimes she notices things that form a pattern,
a pattern that otherwise would pass unasserted — this

rhythm of the parts or moments clattering into
alignment can seem glacial & sedated or creepily

accelerated, a set of dance steps sped up
in re-run, which you can watch again &

again to confirm how to make your own
body take part in the intricate, lovely, social

ritual that sets out some sanctioned, unfrightening form
of intimacy that will wreck no one's soul-heart.

The body will look intact long enough to
start functioning as such; you'll decide if you

are a decent bike worth riding or need
to hide out paralyzed under a huge canopy

of branches & leaves, like yours, dear birch,
& plead to God a bolt of breath

hits you square in the diaphragm. You'll decide
if an hour or ten is enough time

to play dead. You'll get moving again, she
thinks, when the wind slips in & strokes

you head to toe & when the skin
of your person shimmers as if, in a

strange overnight miracle, it has rebuilt itself out
of an entire fresh batch of perfect molecules,

& settled upon you, &, in one smooth
sweep, pulled you upright.

Aug 25

The day begins with a spurious foray onto
Facebook, & the composition of a lengthy, mannered

post, then its erasure, & this process repeated
three or four times, as she moves back

into a desire to think away from that
audience. She hijacks an excerpt to deploy in

this other, less instantaneous forum, sensing your limbs
moving within the leaves.

For this summer she has *a beautiful place*
to make writing, to feel gratitude & an

optimism. No, not yet, but it is moving
in that direction, or several, or swirling updrafts,

or smooth dives, or both at the same
time as a pirouette with the loud words

Fuck R rattling... *rattling in the soft box*
of thought I am stuffing into this device.

& Maybe, she thinks, there's nothing as erotic
as a sentence refusing to erase its extravagant

longing for loud words in the soft-stuffed box
of thought.... What she places on Facebook is

this:

> The. Loud. Words.
> In. The. Soft. Box.
> Of. Thought. We. Are. Stuffing.
> Into. This. Device. Because.
> Why. Not.

Noon. One of the things she is noticing
is how she is making R into a

muse, in much the same way N became
a muse, & S had been a muse,

& before that, & after them both, how
X was a muse. She writes across pain

of feeling rejection, of imaging & imagining herself
to be spurned by someone because this is

an anxious vibrant space of feeling magical, perhaps,
of sensing a capacity in herself to shore-up

her self-esteem as someone who can write &
think intelligently & is therefore desirable: If only

the muse-love could hear inside her head, or
read her on the page, they would catapult

back to her — maybe that's the strategy/belief system

at play.

Or maybe it isn't ever about a reconciliation,
but about plot, & dramatic tension. What's the

inciting event? A near break up, a hanging-on-the-precipice
of trust about to shatter — will it? Won't

it? She lived in this tension her whole
childhood — would they have a final retort of

cataclysmic proportion & would one then leave (for
good), & their family be ruined? & Who

was responsible for this state of emergency? Did
one parent blame the other, although to her

both seemed like reliable, equally loving, adults (toward
the children) — but wasn't the first an expert

at pushing the other away? Had each grown
expecting to be rejected, scorned, because their parents

were unhappy with their physical appearance or personality?
All this conjecture; she doesn't know any of

what it was really like to be the
young people her parents were in their families.

She guesses at it, makes a case to
explain her own psyche. But it's all a

massive grope, a construction, a thing easy to
get confident about, as if the self can

be explained. Managed. She's sinking into so many
clogged patterns right now — the negative pattern of

conjuring rejection & the related positive pattern of
using that rejection to generate a burst of

creative composition. She can hear herself here in
her little studio, alone; part of crouching in

this cage is feeling safe about critiquing the
authority who has placed her here. It is

all very young — blaming the bad parent for
hurting her, sweet child.

        & There's that scene that comes to mind
of being spanked, her small body overturned on

their lap, in her bedroom, feeling arms holding
her down hard-slapping her bum to punish. For

what? She can't remember. She only remembers this
scene happening once, when she was somewhere between

seven & ten, she has no idea, for
she was quite a slight figure throughout those

years. How young does a child need be
to feel being spanked erotic? Is it very

young pre-sexual imprint, or a later prepubescent threshold
kind of imprint? She doesn't know. But she

does know that she has liked asking R
to be physically intense with her, has liked

asking her to slap her, or brace her,
has found her enjoyment being pinned down arousing.

Or maybe all these responses are ways she
activates her mental & emotional sexuality, to involve

psychology as more of a turn on than
touch of bodies alone. But no, she has

wildly enjoyed R's body, both how it looks
& how she moves within it, & displays

herself, how present she is within her body.
So much more than N or S — Christ!

Those two cerebellums! She'd loved so passionately. So
it felt, & then, in each case, after

three years it all dissipated like a made-up
game, like a pantomime where the director calls

Cut & it is over — all the pretending.
Two relationships mostly imagined, epistolary, giving her address

a direction.

She smells the air & breathes. Perfume from
the neighbours' baskets of fresh peaches infiltrates her

patio. Several small dogs pass in the lane,
their leashes jangling, their ribcages flitting past fence

slats. Young customers pool around the doors to
the brewery, sharing a joint. She can picture

what her children are busy with, away from
the house, earning money. She lifts her face

toward your lilting white-grey arms, dear birch, foraging
for emotional logic. She senses her shored-up, accusatory

stance toward R, toward her stated plans to
have whatever sexual activity she wishes. Her hands

fidget as if the blood is moving improperly.
She knows she is treating R as though

she's disloyal & unethical — but R's never said
anything to deny what she wants. She just

entered this bearing of feeling attachment & then
feeling deferred, of blaming R for her pain.

Granted, R then began playing the part, seeming
callous and absent.

All that sounds so easy to de-fuse — but
it isn't. There's a long, deep, she would

even say "pathological" bearing in her, toward recreating
this scene of betrayal that places her &

the lover in a heightened drama of deciding
to continue or end the attachment. It's a

hook, a V shape in an upper branch,
a place for birds & squirrels to make

noise, to vetch. She thinks the rawer factor
is that she & R haven't really attached

to each other, & despite that, they have
a vibrant honesty & intimacy when they're having

sex. Much of this waters down significantly when
they are together & even comes near to

dissolving when they're staving off being in phone
or text or email conversation. It's almost like

they don't know each other, as if they've
had one or two encounters, as if there's

no history between them. Or at least no
enduring narrative between them. Maybe both of them

are too wounded, or unwilling, or beyond really
sharing themselves with each other, or anyone.

Aug 26

Awake to streetcar & subway railyard squeals that
continue with cling-clangs & aural squalor for long

moments on end. It's a whistling as much
as it is a dragging, an against-grade hoisting

& an intake of wheezed breath that doesn't
stop, like a wind that begins to suck

the object world into its vortex. & There
the cicadas. There the exhaust fan like a

box of stomach churn. & Then, late in
the game, there the faint voices next door

of the parents & babies, & the miraculously
articulate toddler, in morning discretion, all is set

in place, all is buzzing, in every direction.

She is impatient, though. She needs motion &
to displace her mind with the upswing of

going somewhere else, to be on the move,
to slide away from the hard dock of

these feelings for R, these recognitions of how
what they shared is ending, or is ended.

She is disappointed. Now too she wonders about
how much the anniversary of death has to

do with today's process. Her mother died on
the 21st, but was her funeral the 26th,

or 27th? — she has to consult the obituary
(it turns out to be the 28th).

　　　　But there was the interim procedure of her
cremation which she could not bring herself to

attend & which meant her sibling went as
the only sentry. How could she have let

family be alone in that? She was terrified
of the fire — the image-world of witnessing just

a crate go into a mouth of flame.
Maybe that's what the railyard soundscape is, such

an alchemy, of watching the box that holds
your mother's body be fed into fire. Anyway,

she couldn't go. So her sibling went alone
& reported back to her, after, that it

had really happened & was done.

Her contribution had been to choose her parent's
final outfit, one part paisley exuberance, one part

uni-colour steadiness & pragmatism. She can't remember now,
or she is confused suddenly, whether it was

the paisley shirt, or the skirt — all her
issues with muddled memory seem like so much

stupidity, such a deficit in her cognition. On
so many counts she simply has no recalled

evidence of how events & objects really "were" —
so much is obliterated & scrambled — like a

perfectly complex puzzle momentarily finished to perfection, to
distinct solution, then a breaking of the whole

into a mess of all the small parts,
placed in a small black bag with drawstring

collar, & a pseudo-suede nap, that you tuck
away in a pocket somewhere knowing you'll never

find the motivation to reconstruct the whole, ever
again. Like a tube of ash matter of

your mother, given by the funeral director directly
to your palm, with a quick handshake &

a gaze that slides off the side of
your head.

Like that sliding, she has sidled into the
second person, removed herself from the macabre imagery

as if to make a space for a
reader who may relate more than they might

wish — instead of saying clearly that it is
herself with the tacky plastic vial of ash,

that she still lacks instinct to "spread" its
contents anywhere, & can't imagine opening the lid

to verify anything is inside — she didn't see
the bonfire & can push away the verdict.

Three years — not so long, really. Only three
years without a mother, her mother.

Against that, losing R begins to feel inconsequential.
Their entire acquaintance unfolded within just one year.

She hadn't known her before — she was one
of the persons to enter her life after

her mother died. Even this seems to stun
her, like a hot jolt of venom from

a garden's bug — a red welt begins — an
urge to tear at the spot of skin

suddenly visible against the field of the whole
body: New people continue to arrive into a

life after the most significant bodies, the ones
that made life possible, & accompanied, have moved

on. It is "reasonable" to predict there are
many new persons still to arrive, that one

or two of them may become the essential
family of her future.

The most important phrase of her mother's mothering
of her was "You will always have people

who love you." It might have been "People
will always love you, M," or "You will

always be loved," or "There will always be
people"; Now she can't make her voice exactly

delivering the phrase come into unquestionable focus — but
her voice is here, the two words "always"

& "love," & her name. She had been
sitting on the living room couch, the one

with white & large mauve floral soft cotton
upholstery, & she was broken by a young

lover with whom she'd been obsessed, someone her
friends considered unworthy, & she was crumpled into

the corner of the couch, desperately sad — completely
shadowed in the abandonment she felt — & her

mother came in the large room & walked
directly to her & sat next to her

& put her hands on her. This is
one of two scenes of this sort from

her whole remembered life (the other involved her
mother hugging her despite the discovery that she

had head lice), with her mother's body pulling
her to her, holding her.

She wonders if she has yet said the
thing to any of her three children that

will work as a healing talisman after she
is dead three years & they feel themselves

to be broken at the edge of anyone
new ever arriving in their future.

She has already coalesced for each of them
into sequences of essential scenes & memories, with

fixed outlines & illusions of floating up from
the continuity of having been mothered. Sometimes she

is vain, & believes she has been a
"better" mother to them than her mother was

to her. She lays silent bets with herself
that they will have something euphonious inside their

mind when it comes to whether they were
loved & are lovable in the world, not

the protracted wailing squeals without language that strain
& almost split in her internal bandstand.

            But it is too much to know. Her
children each have private, utterly restricted, irrefutable concepts

of their own lived identity. & There were
enough unresolved batshit-crazy scenes when she stood shaking

at the limits of her capacity to mother
that will have broken off as phantoms in

their recall, that may persist as flashes of
being abandoned, & shattered, & ground down to

morsels of noise. We all have to acquire
language & bear three years — including at least

six months in utero — where everything, not just
consciousness, was oily soundscape, eerie, irregular, matched by

quickening & slowing palpitations throughout the body as
we float within waves of maternal bloodgush &

her amphitheatrical pulse, her hum & her emotions,
moving like wind throughout the tree of her

body, day & night.

Having sex, with a loved lover, is closest
to this sensory amplitude. She felt awash with

R many times; she was a place around
her, & she felt inside her, & slid

into sound & movement with her body &
perceived a world with shape &, shapeless, touch

inside & outside — a shifting sentience. She was
being loved, as her mother had predicted.

Aug 27, 2009

Birch

Bitter the word. Bitter, meadow I am walking in.
Bitter breeze filters through birch foliage.
Each leaf flinches. Cherish me today
For I am a vetch crisp & uncorrected.

I have too-white bark that peels from my core.
I am leaving my bitter body, its sturdy V-shapes
& nodding flourishes. I am curling like a fetus
Into the non-birch world. Enough I have had

Of my paper-skinned nature. My thin, ever-springlike ensemble
Leading you to love me for my fragility. Forget it.
I turn & chafe. I misbeget the fruit of the other trees.
Turdish shapes, all of you. A filament of sun widows me,

My head about to gasp, my crown flickers too green.
I am waiting, waiting for night. When it comes, all
My glowing turrets will be unbidden but lit, settled
In their aura. The night will gentle me. My shine

Will make friends with you until dawn. Why? Just to make
you ache, just
To canopy your gaze, to gash your advances. Opponent, do not
Touch the skin before dusk. Don't touch me
Without the dark, for I am a bitter touch.

Aug 28

She wants now to listen beyond this patio
& beyond the fenced backyard around it, beyond

the physical reach of you, dear birch, &
beyond the specific vantage of this writing moment.

The great beyond. Really, it is the place
where *you* are. What happened to you last

night at the intersection four blocks from your
house; Were you enroute from one space to

another, not quite arrived, in the middle of
a stroll you know well, when something unusual

occurred & you felt yourself turning slowly to
allow your view of the "happening" as your

streetcar trudged past it? Did you glimpse any
bodies being moved from the wreckage?

She saw two, first from the small crushed
car, then from the space between two cars

at the curb. It was all in shadow,
outside the floodlit cone from a police cruiser's

headlamps, aimed at the convenience store parking lot
where a group of figures was being held

in line. Several cops extended their arms with
just the left wrist rotating side to side,

the silhouette of their fingers flicking toward the
lot's eastern edge, as if choreographed by Lucinda

Childs. People complied. It was weirdly quiet.

        You got off two stops later & walked
up the dark street, under swaying tree branches,

beneath the movement of thousands of dark-green leaves,
each flickering & ushering a small scrape into

the night air. You thought of the birch
in your backyard & how, in the morning,

in daylight, you would sit at the ironwork
patio table & write about the past, the

immediate past, which was gateway to the distant,
acute, specific past.

        You were always, or often, writing about your
own past, which was soaked in the floodlight

from your own headlamp. Outside the bright yellow
cone, there were unnoticed objects & events. There

were people, & shadowed cops — the arms of
the State — & others cleaning & caring &

moving bodies that, on that night, had fallen
somehow, or been hit, or were dissembling.

Each of those persons, even, or especially, the
dissembling ones, had on their own headlamp. Each

was seeing a wedge of information lit up
like a stage show, a travelling carnival, a

funnel of floodlit perception. If you begin to
look closely, you could see evidence of how

this was true. We were in a mine,
every one of us wore a miner's headlamp,

& it was always, permanently, on. The glare
of it, however, made it difficult to discern

the others. You had to correct for distortion,
like when parking a trailer & relying on

the rearview mirror jutting from the left side,
beyond that strange space between the square window

& the triangular window. A trick in calculation
was essential. Otherwise, you'd back into a body,

out of nowhere, & the light would vanish.

When the wind picks up, it makes your
entire canopy, dear birch, thrash like a teenager

in a mosh pit. While this goes on
a twenty-foot delivery truck backs down the lane,

with its purple-blue beeping alarm loudly signalling to
the neighbourhood that no one can see anyone

else & that it's your own fault if
you don't understand this. Your high leaves are

shimmying & rattling against the breeze, & if
she dials up her listening she can enter

a virtual synthesis with a globe ten metres
above her of flapping, sussurant, wind-engorged foliage, now

competitively answered by the cicada choral garland, zinging
& drilling overhead at the same pitch as

your load of wind.

To hear any of this, & certify its
avant-garde brilliance, she has to sit in the

iron chair & appear to everyone in her
immediate & remote past like a layabout on

perennial holiday. No other person will attach the
word "labour" to her body. The delivery truck

driver will gun the engine & leave, moving
forward this time, droning rhinoceros. & The east

neighbour will arrive on her back deck with
a contractor for a boisterous renovation consult where

the agreement is struck for new skirting, step
tops, new decking, rebuild this, this, this, make

it look new — might as well — whether relatticing
is part of the contract is left to

the renovator's discretion. The neighbour's dog is going
ballistic inside the sealed cell of her kitchen;

The builder is vying for extra improvements. Bright
yellow beams of light glaring from the communion

of their headlamps are fanning through the fence
& strobing onto this patio, & they are

peering through slats as if her writing body
doesn't exist, & the builder pronounces the general

figure "ten thousand," then, "No: *$10,850.*" He hopes
he is competitive. The neighbour is poker-voiced. Their

meeting dissembles. Breeze, you, dear birch, cicadas, the
wind chimes, the GO train & several sirens

all in concert whip up a furious crescendo,
& she is smelling the wide green lawn

at her family's cottage where labour must always
appear to be in progress & this labour

must involve the timely replacing of older things
with newer things, which she understands is beneficial.

Nothing in this text will be beneficial. You
exist in her dreaming, alongside a large cat,

floral memories of a couch, & lunchtime bicycling.
This environmental exercise is extraneous.

Last night she saw R & repaired some
of their boycott. They sat on a pair

of poplar stumps deep in R's courtyard, in
darkness, under the dense span of a beautiful

variegated tree that she recently confirmed was a
young horse chestnut. They spoke in low tones,

laughed softly. Some negotiation of their attachment was
jiggled into place, like the laying of much

of the perimeter & a few obvious puzzle
pieces onto the vinylled surface of a card

table agreed to remain set up in a
quiet corridor, as in her mother's nursing home

three summers ago. You could always come by
to insert a few small shapes into the

gradually forming larger shapes. You had to be
patient with all the blank areas — they got

to drift & become more or less discernible,
& occasionally a few random guess-pieces would be

positioned as free floaters unattached to any of
the puzzle structure in process, but laid in,

made operational. All that could be said was
that they were imagined to belong on the

table, in the general terrain of part of
the puzzle, that a soft pitch was being

played, which could also be seen as courageous,
visionary. Attachment was the puzzle; monogamy was the

blank field, or "sky." There seemed no reason
to ever complete the image — it was agreed

that cloud-shaped floater fields filled in with nothing
would have a place in the larger shape.

Something was agreed about kindness. Each of them
narrated a few new, additional remembered events from

their lives when in their early twenties; They
listened to versions of encounters that must be

recognized as fictional gestures toward building a new
skirting, or decking, or lattice-work between them.

There's less bitterness in her voice today. When
she listens, she is listening, beyond it. Somebody

else's life went under a car last night;
hers was hauled out from her own chest.

It's a sort of labour that can't be
written up on an invoice. Or it can:

bp Nichol's sound poems of the seventies &
eighties actually existed as scores — ululation with measures

of silence, crushed words stuttered as a triplet
of the consonant *f* alternated with a palpitated

d, a branch of fluttered yet upper-case *r*'s
& the soaking outrush of the dipthong *oy*.

Nichol was proposing a sort of music for
anyone's walk home on a dark night; for

any speaker's paralyzed otherness. He was her teacher,
& her verifier. You could make poems from

sound; you could love in a complex, contradictory,
inchoate reach. If your mother dies, you are

invited to grieve for three years, & more.
You will not close the puzzle, ever, &

that's better than closing it, ever.

Notes

This text was initially composed out of doors on Ivy Avenue, in the east end of Toronto, in a rented backyard space arrayed around a supremely vivid birch.

Initials & details are promiscuous.

Acknowledgement to Laurence Steven, & Your Scrivener Press, for publishing "Birch" in *Welling*, 2010.

Acknowledgement to Bookhug for publishing my chapbook *Retreat Diary*, 2004, & to Coach House Books for including "Retreat Diary" & the longer ten-word-per-line "counted" poems "Waiting" & "Lucent" in *Sooner*, 2005.

Warm thanks to my terrific editor Jim Johnstone, Aimee Parent Dunn, Ellie Hastings and everyone at Palimpsest Press for your steadfast care and creative generosities. Thank you to Maureen Hynes and Stephanie Bolster for kindly weighing this poem cycle in advance.

Thanks to my family and to friends and colleagues, and to persons I have loved and love, and will love.

Margaret Christakos is attached to this earth. An award-winning author and Chalmers fellow, she has published eleven collections of poetry, a novel (*Charisma*, 2000), and an intergenre memoir (*Her Paraphernalia: On Motherlines, Sex, Blood, Loss & Selfies*, 2016). Recent books include *Space Between Her Lips: The Poetry of Margaret Christakos* (a Selected, in 2017), the chapbook *Retreat Diary 2019*, and the poetry collection *charger* (2020). She perennially explores — as a poet, intermedia image-maker, sometimes event-builder, and oft creative writing mentor, and has been writer-in-residence with five Canadian universities. Born and raised in Sudbury, she lives in Toronto.